The Shot Heard 'Round the World:
The Beginnings of the American Revolution

Edited by Jeanne Munn Bracken

© Discovery Enterprises, Ltd.
Lowell, Massachusetts

© Discovery Enterprises, Ltd., Lowell, MA 1995

ISBN 1-878668-32-3 paperback edition
Library of Congress Catalog Card Number 94-71898

10   9   8   7   6   5   4   3   2   1

Printed in the United States of America

Subject Reference Guide:
Cataloging in Publication   D973.3
Concord, Battle of (1775)
Lexington, Battle of (1775)
United States – History – Colonial Period, ca. 1600-1775
United States – History – Personal Narratives

Acknowledgments

The following books provided original source materials as noted:

Annals of America, vol. 2 (Abigail Adams and "Yankee Doodle")

Rankin, Hugh F., *The American Revolution*
(Amos Barrett, Lt. John Barker and General Thomas Gage)

Scheer, George F. and Hugh F. Rankin, *Rebels and Redcoats*
(Lord Hugh Percy, Ethan Allen, Jocelyn Feltham,
John Trumbull, and Peter Brown.)

Voices from America's Past,
edited by Richard B. Morris and James Woodress
(George Hewes, Thomas Paine and John Adams)

We Were There! edited by Vincent J-R Kehoe
(Elizabeth Clarke, Martha Moulton)

I am also grateful to my colleagues at the
Lincoln (MA) Public Library, the Boston Public Library, the
Concord Public Library, the Fletcher Memorial Library in
Westford, MA, the Reuben Hoar Library in Littleton, MA;
Susan Paju of the Acton Memorial Library and Tina Blood of
the Morrill Memorial Library, Norwood, MA.

Dedication

*This book is dedicated to the
Littleton Electric Light Department
for cooperation above and beyond the call of
duty during a period of planned power outages
while this book was being finished.*

Table of Contents

Ready!

Seeds of Revolution

The United States of America came about almost by accident. Settlers came to the shores of the New World for many reasons. Some sought wealth, others religious freedom. Some came as debtors or prisoners, others as servants or slaves. They came from England, France, Holland, and Spain, to scattered settlements mostly along the Atlantic Coast. None came with the idea of creating a new nation with a new form of government.

The various European colonies were actually quite different in their origins. The Spanish colonies were formed directly by the government. In spite of their distance from the Mother Country, they were tightly controlled by the crown and by the Roman Catholic Church.

The French allowed devout Roman Catholics to colonize portions of the New World north and west of the English colonies.

New Amsterdam was settled by a private firm, the Dutch West India Company, authorized by the Dutch government. This was the shortest-lived of them all, conquered by England in 1664 and renamed New York.

The seeds of the United States of America, however, were planted in English colonial soil. Despite the long and often terrible ocean voyage, the English population in America grew.

Many in the southern areas were brought as indentured servants to work the farms and tobacco plantations. The colonies expanded until there was thirteen in all.

Unlike the Spanish and French, the earliest English colonies were not directly governed by the crown or by any church. The English colonists therefore had more independence from the start than did those settling in the name of Spain or France. They were authorized by the government but were actually formed by private companies seeking profit. These companies expected to gain from shipping people and goods to the colonies and back to England. This system had proven profitable in parts of the world where there were valuable mineral resources and a large native workforce to exploit. North America, as they discovered, did not have gold or potential slaves. What the settlers found instead was good farmland, timber, and, in the early years, disease and starvation. In fact, the Virginia Company, which staked its claim as Jamestown colony as early as 1607, went broke in 1624. Tobacco became the major export from the "southern colonies", too late to save the company but forming a lifeblood for the Virginia colony itself.

Another major difference among the English colonies was the religion of the settlers. Most were Protestants, but not from a unified group like the powerful Roman Catholic Church of Spain and France. From England came a variety of Protestant religions: the Pilgrims in Plymouth, the Puritans in Boston and Connecticut, the English Roman Catholics in Maryland, the Quakers in Pennsylvania, Roger Williams' splinter group of dissident Puritans in Rhode Island. There was little to tie these groups into a unified whole, which would have been much easier to govern from afar.

The growing English colonies had frequent difficulties with the Indians, the French, and the Spanish, and they argued amongst themselves as well. Still, by 1700 they were far more successful than their neighbors in North America. The British government had given power, political favors, and the rights to vast parcels of land to private companies. It was time to collect. The private companies founded to exploit New World wealth were brought under tight control from London. Royal governors were sent to represent the King in the English colonies.

To increase profits, Parliament passed laws ("acts") requiring that even non-English commodities such as rum from the West Indies must be shipped to the colonies by way of England. Tobacco, rice and other products from the colonies had to be sent by way of England no matter what the final destination might be.

More and more tax collectors and customs officers were sent to America to enforce these laws. Their rule was not particularly strong, however. From the earliest days, the colonists had chosen representatives and held meetings to rule themselves. These elected assemblies weakened the power of the royal governors. The settlers for the most part continued to manage and govern their own affairs.

Life in the colonies was also quite different from that in England. The Mother Country had a wealthy upper class, with estates and titles, art and music, and great cities. They also had a huge, poor, lower class living in slums.

The English colonists, on the other hand, were generally comfortable. There were, to be sure, some families with wealth and status, but most of the white colonists at least owned their own farmlands. The majority fell into the trade or craftsman class—shop-keepers, candlemakers and carpenters. They had plenty to eat after the first starving years were behind them. This, too, set them apart from the sometimes famine-stricken England. Historian Gordon S. Wood suggests that "(the) American colonists. . .probably enjoyed the highest standard of living in the world." Yet many Europeans considered the colonists uncultured savages.

As life in the colonies became more settled and stable, the English immigrants were joined by neighbors from Scotland, Ireland and Germany. Slaves were imported as servants and especially as laborers for the southern plantations; blacks made up a quarter of the population by the 1770s.

The population increased. The few struggling colonists fighting illness and a hostile climate in Plymouth and Jamestown comprised almost 20% of the population of the British world—two million strong by 1770. (By comparison, the 1990 population of Boston and its suburbs was about two million!) Nearly half of the powerful British shipping industry involved the movement of goods either to or from the American continent.

The British government grew alarmed at the growing power of that rag-tag, uncivilized bunch living an ocean away from Parliament's authority.

At the same time that the New World was growing, England, France and Spain had been struggling for power in Europe. Now, in the mid-18th century, the battleground shifted to North America. France, allied with native Americans and the Spanish, built forts inland to lay claim to the vast middle of the continent. The French and Indian War (also called The Seven Years' War) followed. King George III had wealth and a large colonial population behind him. By 1763 his troops had defeated his European enemies, laying claim to almost the entire eastern half of North America. England had indeed gained a brilliant jewel for her crown.

This victory did not come cheap. The French and Indian War had thrown the British deeply into debt. The expense was not yet over. Rather than call the British army home after the peace treaty was signed, the soldiers were left in America. They were expected to police the newly acquired territories and to protect the Indians from the colonists, who were eager to move farther into the interior. The war had been staggeringly expensive, but the cost of peace was worse.

Not surprisingly, the British government looked to the prosperous colonies for help in paying their massive war debts and in financing the peace in the expanded territories. The colonists, used to going about their affairs with little interference from England, were not easily subdued. Much of the pressure squeezed Boston, with its free-thinking colonial traditions. The colonists resisted, and finally they revolted.

Aim!

The Pressure on Boston

In Boston, the pressure was on. The Bostonians especially resisted the customs fees placed on imports by the Crown. John Hancock, well-known patriot and wealthy shipper, imported a shipload of Madeira wine into Boston in mid-1768 but refused to pay the taxes. His sloop "Liberty" waited in the harbor to unload. Customs officers were captured and locked up in the ship while the wine was illegally unloaded. In retaliation, the "Liberty" was seized and anchored in the harbor next to the British warship "Romney." A protesting mob frightened the officials, who fled first to the safety of the "Romney" and then to Castle William on a harbor island.

Ann Hulton was an excellent witness to the happenings in Boston. She lived with her brother Henry, the Commissioner of Customs in Boston from 1767 to 1776. It was his duty to collect the taxes. Hulton was a frequent target of the angry mobs and the family was forced more than once to leave their comfortable home and flee for safety to Castle William.

Letters of a Loyalists Lady presents a royalist's view of the events in Boston leading up to the Revolution. Her writings have been somewhat edited for modern readers:

> You will be surprised to hear how we were obliged to take refuge on board the *Romney* man of war lying in Boston Harbour. Mrs. Burch at whose house I was, had frequently been alarmed with the Sons of Liberty sur-

rounding her house with most hideous howlings as the Indians, when they attack an enemy, to many insults and outrages She had been exposed since her arrival and threatened with greater violences. She had removed her most valuable (possessions) and held herself in readiness to depart at an hour's notice. The occasion soon happened. . .we soon found that the mobs here are very different from those in Old England. . .these Sons of Violence after attacking houses, breaking windows, beating, stoning and bruizing several Gentlemen belonging to the Customs, the Collector mortally and burning his boat. . . All was ended with a speech from one of the leaders, concluding thus, "We will defend our Liberties and property, by the Strength of our Arm and the Help of our God. . ." This is a specimen of the Sons of Liberty, of whom no doubt you have heard, and will hear more. . . .

That evening Saturday we set off in a barge under a convoy of Man of War Boats, with Marines, their bayonets fixed, to the "Romney," a fifty gun ship of war, lying ready in the Harbour. On the 21st (June) we removed to this castle by the Governor's permission. This was a Scene you will believe quite new to me, and indeed the series of events since leaving Old England appears romantic. (June 30, 1768)

The refugees, while living in some comfort, remained on the Island for several weeks until they felt safe enough to return to their homes. After the "Boston Massacre" on March 5, 1770, they again spent five months at the island fortress.

In reality, what we know as the Boston Massacre was not a "massacre" at all. On the evening of March 5, an angry mob gathered on the streets of Boston and taunted some British soldiers patrolling there, threatening them with stones and snowballs. The officer in charge, Captain William Preston, tried to avoid further violence, but someone fired a shot. The frightened soldiers then shot into the crowd. Five colonists were killed. The soldiers and Preston were tried in court for murder and, defended by patriot John Adams, were acquitted of the charge, although two were found guilty of lesser crimes. Ann Hulton again:

> . . .We never thought ourselves more safe from the Sons of Violence than at present. . . .the impartial trial and honorable acquital of Captain Preston and the Soldiers has the most happy effect, it has exposed the conduct of the faction, and opened the eyes of the people in general, convinced them that they have been deceived by false opinions, and false representations of facts. It has ascertained the right of Self Defence. . . . Many persons have told us that we shall never receive any more insults or attacks here. . ." *(December 21, 1770)*

The optimistic Miss Hulton spoke too soon.

Tensions built in the colonies with the imposition of the Tea Act in 1773. The British repealed the export tax on tea in order to help the struggling British East India Company. This allowed the import of tea into America at prices below those the colonists had to pay when they imported tea themselves. The angry merchants protested with the Boston Tea Party on the night of December 16, 1773. Colonist George Hewes was one of the "Indians" who took part in the midnight raid:

> The tea destroyed was contained in three ships, lying near each other at what was called at that time Griffin's wharf, and were surrounded by armed ships of war. The commanders had publicly declared that if the rebels, as they were pleased to style the Bostonians,

should not withdraw their opposition to the landing of the tea before a certain day, the 17th day of December, 1773, they should on that day force it on shore under cover of their cannon's mouth.

. . . It was now evening, and I immediately dressed myself in the costume of an Indian, equipped with a small hatchet, which I and my associates denominated the tomahawk, and a club. After having painted my face and hands with coal dust in the shop of a black-smith, I (went) to Griffin's wharf, where the ships lay that contained the tea.

. . . They divided us into three parties, for the purpose of boarding the ships which contained the tea at the same time. . . . The commander of the division to which I belonged, as soon as we were on board the ship. . . ordered me to go to the captain and demand of him the keys to the hatches and a dozen candles. I made the demand accordingly, and the captain promptly replied, and delivered the articles; but requested me at the same time to do no damage to the ship or rigging. We then were ordered by our commander to open the hatches and take out all the chests of tea and throw them overboard, and we immediately proceeded to execute his orders, first cutting and splitting the chests with our tomahawks, so as thoroughly to expose them to the effects of the water.

In about three hours from the time we went on board, we had thus broken and thrown overboard every tea chest to be found in the ship, while those in the other ships were disposing of the tea in the same way, at the same time. We were surrounded by British armed ships, but no attempt was made to resist us. . . . No disorder took place during that transaction, and it was observed at the time that the stillest night ensued that Boston had enjoyed for many months.

Ann Hulton's view of the Boston Tea Party was of course quite different.

> You will perhaps expect me to give you some accounting of the state of Boston and late proceedings here but really the times are too bad and the scenes too shocking for me to describe. I suppose you will have heard long before this arrives of the fate of the Tea. . . .The Commissioners of the Customs and the Tea (owners) were obliged to seek refuge at the Castle. (About three weeks after the Tea Party) my brother returned home and the other commissioners left the castle. The violent fury of the people having subsided a little. *(January 31, 1774)*

Music and poetry commonly reflect or remember important events. This poem formed the lyrics to a song that likened England to a mother and America to her daughter. Neither the author nor the date it was written is known, but it was popular by the time of the Civil War and was probably known long before that.

Revolutionary Tea

There was an old lady lived over the sea,
And she was an Island Queen;
Her daughter lived off in a new country,
With an ocean of water between.
The old lady's pockets were full of gold,
But never contented was she,
So she called on her daughter to pay her a tax
Of three pence a pound on her tea,
Of three pence a pound on her tea.

"Now mother, dear mother," the daughter replied,
"I shan't do the thing that you ax;
I'm willing to pay a fair price for the tea,
But never the three penny tax."

Boston Tea Party, artist unknown

"You shall," quoth the mother, and reddened with rage,
"For you're my own daughter, you see,
And sure 'tis quite proper the daughter should pay
Her mother a tax on her tea,
Her mother a tax on her tea."

And so the old lady her servant called up,
And packed off a budget of tea;
And eager for three pence a pound, she put in
Enough for a large family.
She ordered her servants to bring home the tax,
Declaring her child should obey,
Or old as she was, and almost woman grown,
She'd half whip her life away,
She'd half whip her life away.

The tea was conveyed to the daughter's door,
All down by the ocean's side;
And the bouncing girl poured out every pound
In the dark and boiling tide.
And then she called out to the Island Queen,
"Oh, mother, dear mother," quoth she,
"Your tea you may have when 'tis steeped enough,
But never a tax from me,
But never a tax from me."

Fire!

To Lexington and Concord

By the spring of 1775, affairs in the colonies and especially in Boston had come to a head. The British had spies everywhere and knew that the citizens were gathering arms and ammunition in the event of an outbreak of hostilities. The Colonists had spies, too, and knew perfectly well that the British might march into the countryside to seize the hidden supplies. Paul Revere was one of the more active colonists, riding hither and yon that spring, passing messages to the colonists in the days before telephones. No doubt his most famous ride was the one on the evening of April 18, 1775, when he rode into the Middlesex countryside to warn the towns of Lexington (where Sam Adams and John Hancock were staying) and Concord (where many of the supplies were hidden) that the British were on the march.

Silversmith Paul Revere left three accounts of his famous ride, two eyewitness depositions given shortly after the events in 1775 and a letter written about 25 years later, from which the following is taken. We may forgive Revere for his colonial grammar and spelling, which is reproduced here as he wrote it.

It is ironic to note that, despite the care taken that the Committee's activities should not be discovered, Dr. Benjamin Church turned out to be a British spy. The colonists suspected that the British were going to make a move into the countryside because boats had been repaired and some of the soldiers had been taken off regular duty, the better to be prepared for a special march. Something was clearly in the spring wind. "One if by land and two if by sea," from Longfellow's poem about the incident, is well-known. The British had two possible routes to Concord; they could march either by way of the long, thin narrow strip of land called Boston Neck, which was guarded by the British, or they could be carried in boats across the Charles River and march a somewhat shorter, more direct route. As Revere says, the lanterns were never intended as a substitute for riders but were a backup in case the messengers weren't able to get out of Boston at all. William Dawes was sent as a messenger by way of Boston Neck, a different route, in hopes that at least one of them would reach Lexington and Concord. From *Paul Revere's Three Accounts of his Famous Ride*:

> . . .In the fall of 1774 and the winter of 1775, I was one of upwards of thirty. . .who formed ourselves into a Committee for the purpose of watching the Movements of the British Soldiers, and gaining every intelligence of the movements of the Tories. We held our meetings at the Green-Dragon tavern. We were so careful that our meetings should be kept secret, that every time we met, every person swore upon the Bible, that they would not discover any of our transactions, but to Messrs. [John] Hancock, [Samuel] Adams, Doctors [Joseph] Warren, [Benjamin] Church, and one or two more.
>
> . . .On Tuesday evening, the 18th, it was observed, that a number of Soldiers were marching towards the bottom of the Common. About 10 o'Clock, Dr. Warren Sent in great haste for me, and beged that I would immediately Set off for Lexington, where Messrs. Hancock

and Adams were, and acquaint them of the Movement, and that it was thought they were the objects. When I got to Dr. Warren's house, I found he had sent an express by land to Lexington—a Mr. Wm. Daws [Dawes]. . . .I had agreed (beforehand) with a Col. Conant (in Charlestown). . .that if the British went out by Water, we would shew two Lanthorns in the North Church Steeple; and if by Land, one, as a Signal; for we were aprehensive it would be difficult to Cross the Charles River, or git over Boston neck. I left Doctor Warrens, called upon a friend, and desired him to make the Signals. I then went Home, took my Boots and Surtout, and went to the North part of the Town, Where I had kept a Boat; two friends rowed me across the Charles River, a little to the eastward where the Somerset Man of War lay. It was then young flood, the Ship was winding, and the moon was Rising. They landed me on Charlestown side. When I got into Town, I met Col. Conant, and several others; they said they had seen our signals. I told them what was Acting, and went to git me a Horse; I got a Horse of Deacon Larkin.

Paul Revere's Ride, artist unknown

. . . I set off upon a very good Horse; it was then about 11 o'Clock, and very pleasant. After I had passed Charlestown Neck. . . I saw two men on Horse back, under a Tree. When I got near them, I discovered they were British officers. One tryed to git a head of Me, and the other to take me. I turned my horse very quick, and Galloped towards Charlestown neck, and then pushed for the Medford Road. The one who chased me, endeavoring to Cut me off, got into a Clay pond. . . I got clear of him, and went thro Medford, over the Bridge, and up to Menotomy. In Medford, I awaked the Captain of the Minute men; and after that, I alarmed almost every house, till I got to Lexington. I found Messrs. Hancock and Adams at the Rev. Mr. Clark's; I told them my errand and inquired for Mr. Daws; they said he had not been there. I related the story of the two officers, and supposed that He must have been stopped, as he ought to have been there before me. After I had been there about half an Hour, Mr. Daws came; we refreshid our selves, and set off for Concord, to secure the Stores, etc. there. We were overtaken by a young Docter Prescot [Samuel Prescott of Concord], whom we found to be a high Son of Liberty. I told them . . . that it was probable we might be stopped before we got to Concord; . . . I likewise mentioned, that we had better allarm all the Inhabitents till we got to Concord; the young Doctor much approved of it, and said, he would stop with either of us, for the people between that and Concord knew him, and would give the more credit to what we said.

A British advance party spotted the three riders. Prescott, who knew the countryside, escaped and was able to warn Concord and the towns beyond. Revere and Dawes were captured, threatened and eventually turned loose. Revere's borrowed horse was taken for use by a British officer.

In his *Tales of a Wayside Inn*, New England poet Henry Wadsworth Longfellow (1807-1882) immortalized Paul Revere. Yet in comparing the poem to Revere's own recollections, it is clear that Longfellow used "poetic license." Facts are twisted, but the poem certainly has kept Revere in the minds of Americans ever since its publication in 1860, while poor William Dawes has been all but forgotten.

Paul Revere's Ride (excerpt)
[April 18-19, 1775]

Listen, my children, and you shall hear
Of the midnight ride of Paul Revere,
On the eighteenth of April, in seventy-five;
Hardly a man is now alive
Who remembers that famous day and year.

He said to his friend, "If the British march
By land or sea from the town to-night,
Hang a lantern aloft in the belfry arch
Of the North Church tower as a signal light,—
One, if by land, and two, if by sea;
And I on the opposite shore will be,
Ready to ride and spread the alarm
Through every Middlesex village and farm,
For the country folk to be up and to arm."

Then he said, "Good night!" and with muffled oar
Silently rowed to the Charlestown shore,
Just as the moon rose over the bay,
Where swinging wide at her moorings lay
The Somerset, British man-of-war;
A phantom ship, with each mast and spar
Across the moon like a prison bar,

And a huge black hulk, that was magnified
By its own reflection in the tide.

Meanwhile, his friend, through alley and street,
Wanders and watches with eager ears,
Till in the silence around him he hears
The muster of men at the barrack door,
The sound of arms, and the tramp of feet,
And the measured tread of the grenadiers,
Marching down to their boats on the shore.

Then he climbed the tower of the Old North Church
By the wooden stairs, with stealthy tread,
To the belfry-chamber overhead,
And startled the pigeons from their perch
On the somber rafters, that round him made
Masses and moving shapes of shade,—
By the trembling ladder, steep and tall,
To the highest window in the wall,
Where he paused to listen and look down
A moment on the roofs of the town,
And the moonlight flowing over all....

It was one by the village clock,
When he galloped into Lexington.
He saw the gilded weathercock
Swim in the moonlight as he passed.
And the meeting-house windows, blank and bare,
Gaze at him with a spectral glare,
As if they already stood aghast
At the bloody work they would look upon.

It was two by the village clock,
When he came to the bridge in Concord town.
He heard the bleating of the flock,
And the twitter of birds among the trees,
And felt the breath of the morning breeze
Blowing over the meadows brown.

And one was safe and asleep in his bed
Who at the bridge would be first to fall,
Who that day would be lying dead,
Pierced by a British musket-ball.

You know the rest. In the books you have read,
How the British Regulars fired and fled,—
How the farmers gave them ball for ball,
From behind each fence and farmyard wall,
Chasing the red-coats down the lane,
Then crossing the fields to emerge again
Under the trees at the turn of the road,
And only pausing to fire and load.

So through the night rode Paul Revere;
And so through the night went his cry of alarm
To every Middlesex village and farm,
A Cry of defiance and not of fear,
A voice in the darkness, a knock at the door,
And a word that shall echo forevermore!
For, borne on the night-wind of the Past,
Through all our history, to the last,
In the hour of darkness and peril and need,
The people will waken and listen to hear
The hurrying hoof-beats of that steed,
And the midnight message of Paul Revere.

Despite delays in crossing the Charles River, the British troops eventually were on the march—soggy from wading through the marshes, and tired before they were well underway. Before they got far, it was obvious that their "secret" mission had been discovered. Volleys of three shots rang out, a pre-arranged warning signal to the villages and farms. The officers in charge sent back to Boston for reinforcements in case they met with hostility in the countryside, but a series of errors delayed the departure of the second force of British until late in the morning.

For the moment, they were on their own. Minutemen from the town of Lexington gathered at a local tavern shortly after midnight but were sent home by their officers (although many stayed for a draft of hard cider) because conflicting messages suggested that the British were not on the march after all. It wasn't until the King's troops were almost in Lexington that the colonials were called again to Lexington common by the beating of William Diamond's drum.

Consider the dilemma facing the British as they went behind the Meetinghouse and saw several dozen armed men waiting for them. Patroit leaders Sam Adams and John Hancock were staying with Reverend Jonas Clarke. The colonials feared that the redcoats were heading for Lexington to capture them. They had no way of knowing that military governor Thomas Gage had only ordered the troops to go to Concord and seize or destroy the supplies hidden there. Yet here were hostile colonists blocking the road to Concord. The officer in charge of the advance British troops gave conflicting orders; he called to the colonists to disperse, and to lay down their arms and surrender. Under strict orders not to fire, the crowd of Lexington minutemen did indeed begin to break up, but the farmers were not about to give up their weapons.

Suddenly, from a source that will never be known, a shot rang out. The British insisted they did not fire first and that a shot had come from behind a nearby stone wall. By then Paul Revere had gotten back to

Lexington, reported to Hancock and Adams, and was near the common when the first British troops arrived.

> . . .we saw the British very near, upon a full March. We hurried to wards Mr. Clark's House. In our way, we passed through the Militia. There were about 50. When we had got about 100 yards from the meeting-House the British Troops appeard on both sides of the Meeting-House. In their Front was an Officer on Horse back. They made a Short Halt; when I saw, and heard, a Gun fired, which appeared to be a Pistol. Then I could distinguish two Guns, and then a Continual roar of Musquetry. . .

Revere's statement that he had heard a pistol fire was important, because only the British officers were so armed. Whoever fired first, the tired and no doubt hungry British troops began shooting wildly into the crowd. By the time the gunsmoke cleared, eight Ameri-

The action at Lexington, by Darley

cans were dead and several more wounded. The British claimed that the Americans had fired, too, because Major Pitcairn's horse and one soldier had been wounded (although neither seriously). Pitcairn finally managed to get his rampaging troops under control, three cheers for victory rang out across the night-dark common, and the British regrouped for the march to Concord.

Jonas Clarke's house was a beehive of activity that April night. The Clarke family had twelve children and besides Adams and Hancock, two women were staying there: John Hancock's aunt Lydia Hancock and his fiancee Dorothy Quincy. Many years later, Elizabeth Clarke, who was twelve years old at the time, wrote her niece Lucy Allen her recollections of that night. Elizabeth Clarke:

> . . . (it) is sixty-six years since the war began on the Common which I now can see from this window as here I sit writing, and can see, in my mind, just as plain, all the British troops marching off the Common to Concord, and the whole scene, how Aunt Hancock and Miss Dolly Quinsy [Quincy], with their cloaks and bonnets on, Aunt crying and wringing her hands and helping Mother Dress the children, Dolly going round with Father, to hide Money, watches and anything down in the potatoes and up garrett, and then Grandfather Clarke sent down men with carts, took your Mother and all the children but Jonas and me and Sally a Babe six months old. Father sent Jonas down to Grandfather Cook's to see who was killed and what their condition was and, in the afternoon, Father, Mother with me and the Baby went to the Meeting House, there was the eight men that was killed, seven of them my Father's parishioners, one from Woburn, all in Boxes made of

25

four large Boards Nailed up and, after Pa had prayed, they were put into two horse carts and took into the grave yard where your Grandfather and some of the Neighbors had made a large trench, as near the woods as possible, and there we followed the bodies of those first slain, Father, Mother, and I and the Baby, there I stood and there I saw them let down into the ground, it was a little rainey but we waited to see them Covered up with the Clods and then for fear the British should find them, my Father thought some of the men had best Cut some pine or oak bows [boughs] and spread them on their place of burial so that it looked like a heap of Brush.... (April 19, 1841)

After sounding their three cheers ("huzzahs") on Lexington green, the British regrouped and headed for Concord. Many people later wrote or told their stories, and the narrative can be carried by some of them. Amos Barrett was a 23-year-old corporal of the Concord minutemen:

We at Concord heard they was a-coming. The Bell rung at 3 o'clock for an alarm. As I was then a Minuteman, I was soon in town and found my captain and the rest of my company at the post. It wasn't long before there was other minute companies. One company, I believe, of minute men was raised in almost every town to stand at a minute's warning. Before sunrise there was, I believe 150 of us and more of all that was there.

We thought we would go and meet the British. We marched down towards Lexington about a mile and a half, and we see them a-coming. We halted and stayed there until we got within about 100 rods, then we was ordered to about face and marched before (in front of) them with our drums and fifes a-going and also the British (drums and fifes). We had grand music.

Ensign Jeremy Lister, a British officer of the 10th Regiment of Foot, was on the march. As Lister notes, the British leaders stayed in the middle of the village to search for hidden military goods. The British troops fanned out to farms and houses looking for hidden supplies. Some stayed to guard the North Bridge. Jeremy Lister was among them.

> . . .we had not been long in this situation when we saw a large Body of Men drawn up with the greatest regularity and approach'd us seemingly with an intent to attack, when Lt. (Waldron) Kelly who then Commanded our Company with myself thought it most proper to retire from our situation and join the 4th Company which we did, they still approached.

Amos Barrett's company, meanwhile, had passed through the town and was among those waiting on the hill who alarmed Lister. Amos Barrett:

> We marched into town and then over the North Bridge a little more than half a mile, and then on a hill not far from the bridge where we could see and hear what was a-going on.
>
> What the British came out after, was to destroy our stores (supplies) that we had got laid up for our army. There was in the Town House a number of entrenching tools which they carried out and burnt them. At last they said it was better to burn the house, and set fire to them in the house, but our people begged of them not to burn the house. . .There was about 100 barrels of flour in Mr. Hubbard's malt house; they rolled that out and knocked them to pieces and rolled some in the mill pond, which was saved after they was gone.

While minutemen from surrounding towns gathered on the hill where Barrett was standing, most of the townspeople had left Concord. Those on the hill couldn't see what was happening back in the village. Martha Moulton, an elderly widow, was one of those who stayed behind, and her deposition, given later in hopes of getting some financial consideration for her acts, is an almost comic description of events in Concord that morning. It is written in the third person as a legal petition. At that point, the British were still careful to spare any private property they might come across.

. . .on the 19th day of April, 1775, in the forenoon, the town of Concord, wherein I dwell, was beset with an army of regulars, who, in a hostile manner, entered the town, and drawed up in form before the door of the house where I live; and there they continued on the green, feeding their horses within five feet of the door; and about fifty or sixty of them was in and out of the house, calling for water and what they wanted, for about three hours. . . .

(Martha Moulton), being left to the mercy of six or seven hundred armed men, and no person near but an old man of eighty-five years, and myself seventy-one years old, and both very infirm. It may easily be imagined what a sad condition your petitioner must be in. Under these circumstances, your petitioner committed herself. . .as to wait on them, as they called, with water, or what we had,—chairs for Major Pitcairn and four or five more officers,—who sat at the door viewing their men. At length (Moulton) had, by degrees, cultivated so much favor as to talk a little with them. When all on a sudden they had set fire to the great gun-carriages just by the house, and while they were in flames (Moulton) saw smoke arise out of the Town House higher than the ridge of the house. Then (Moulton) did put her life, as it were, in her hand, and ventured to beg of the officers to send some of their men to put out the fire; but they took no notice, only sneered. Your petitioner seeing the Town House on fire, and must in a few minutes be past recovery, did yet venture to expostulate with the officers just by her, as she stood with a pail of water in her hand, begging of them to send, etc. When they only said, "O, mother, we won't do you any harm!" "Don't be concerned, mother," and such like talk. The house still burning, and knowing that all the row of four or five houses, as well as the school-house, was in certain danger, (Moulton) (not knowing but she might provoke them by her insufficient pleading) yet ventured to put as much strength to her arguments as an unfortunate widow could think of; so (Moulton) can safely say that...she was an instrument of saving the Court House, and how much more is not certain, from being consumed, with a great deal of valuable furniture, and at the great risk of her life. At last, by one pail of water after another, they sent and did extinguish the fire....

With Martha Moulton harrassing them, gnat-like, to put out the fire, the British did so. Meanwhile, the colonials gathering on the hill saw the smoke and thought the British were burning the town. It was that smoke that moved them to action. After milling about for some time while more and more Americans arrived on the hill, they decided to march down and protect the village. As they started, the British began to tear planks from the bridge. Some of their own regulars would be stranded on the "wrong" side of the river if the bridge were destroyed, but apparently that was forgotten in the stress of the moment. Both sides had been warned not to fire first.

When they reached Lexington, the British troops were tired, angry and hungry. They lay on the green, "with their tongues hanging out like dogs," one witness said. Their ammunition nearly gone, hounded by fresh colonial troops, and with many miles between them and safety in Boston, their situation was very serious. At that moment, the reinforcements Colonel Smith had requested the night before finally arrived under Lord Hugh Percy. Percy had brought two cannons with him but his ammunition had been delayed, then seized by a half dozen old men in the town of Menotomy (now called Arlington).

After firing a couple of cannon rounds into the village of Lexington and burning some buildings, the British troops regrouped and headed back toward Boston, ever harried by the colonials. The fiercest fighting of the day took place in Menotomy, and by the time the regulars were safely in Charlestown under the protection of the guns of the anchored men of war in the river, they were exhausted. The war had begun.

The Reverend William Emerson died a year later of "camp fever." His grandson, Ralph Waldo Emerson, wrote the now famous "Concord Hymn" for the dedication of a battle monument at the North Bridge on July 4, 1837.

Concord Hymn

By the rude bridge that arched the flood,
   Their flag to April's breeze unfurled,
Here once the embattled farmers stood
   And fired the shot heard round the world.

The foe long since in silence slept;
   Alike the conqueror silent sleeps;

And Time the ruined bridge has swept
　　Down the dark stream which seaward creeps.

On this green bank, by this soft stream,
　　We set today a votive stone;
That memory may their deed redeem,
　　When, like our sires, our sons are gone.

Spirit, that made those heroes dare
　　To die and leave their children free,
Bid time and Nature gently spare
　　The shaft we raise to them and thee.

Most of the British were shocked that the rag-tag colonists had defeated the strongest army in the world in the skirmishes on April 19, 1775. Lord Hugh Percy, who had led the reinforcements that surely saved many British lives on that day, wrote the next morning to Adjutant General Edward Harvey in England:

> Whoever looks upon them as an irregular mob will find himself much mistaken. They have men amongst them those who know very well what they are about, having been employed as Rangers against the Indians and Canadians, and this country being much covered with wood and hilly is very advantageous for their method of fighting.
>
> Nor are several of their men void of a spirit of enthusiasm, as we experienced yesterday, for many of them concealed themselves in houses and advanced within ten yards to fire at me and other officers, though they were morally certain of being put to death themselves in an instant.
>
> You may depend upon it, that as the rebels have now had time to prepare, they are determined to go through with it, nor will the insurrection here turn out so despicable as it is perhaps imagined at home. For my part, I never believe, I confess that they would have attacked

the King's troops or have had the perserverence I found in them yesterday.

Lord Percy was much on the mind of Ann Hulton when she wrote to England shortly after these events. She was not an admirer of the colonists, passing along the rumor that the dead British soldiers had been scalped. In reality, a young lad armed only with a hatchet crossed the North Bridge a little while after the skirmish; when one of the mortally wounded regulars reared up, the frightened boy struck out with his weapon and killed him. None of the other regulars were mutilated at all.

Another source of anger for the British was the American form of fighting, learned, as Percy says, during earlier wars. The regulars were trained to line up in rows in the open. The front troops would fire, then drop to the rear and reload while the next fired, and so on. Ann Hulton:

> The Troops went on to Concord and executed the business they were sent on, and on their return found two or three of their people Lying in the Agonies of Death, scalp'd and their Noses and ears cut off and Eyes bored out—Which exasperated the Soldiers exceedingly —a prodigious number of People now occupying the Hills, woods and Stone Walls along the road. The Light Troops drove some parties from the hills, but all the road being inclosed with Stone Walls Served as a cover to the Rebels, from whence they fired on the Troops still running off whenever they had fired, but still supplied by fresh Numbers. . .
>
> The next day the Country pourd down its Thousands, and at this time from the entrance of Boston Neck at Roxbury round by Cambridge to Charlestown is surrounded by at least 20,000 men. . .We are now

cut off from all communication with the Country and many people must soon perish with famine in this place. Some families have laid in store of Provisions against a Siege. . . . Amidst our distress and apprehension, I am rejoyced our British Hero was preserved, My Lord Percy had a great many and miraculous escapes in the late Action. This amiable Young Nobleman with the Graces which attracts Admiration, possesses the virtues of the heart, and all those qualities form the great Soldier—Vigilent Active, temperate, humane, great Command of temper, fortitude in enduring hardships and fatigue, and Intrepidity in dangers.

The military governor of Massachusetts, Thomas Gage, in writing to England about the events of April 19, 1775, also sent a warning:

They are now spirited up by a rage and enthusiasm as great as ever people were possessed of, and you must proceed in earnest or give the business up. A small body acting in one spot will not avail. You must have large armies, making diversions on different sides to divide their force.

The loss we have sustained is greater than we can bear. Small armies can't afford such losses, especially when the advantage gained tends to little more than the gaining of a post—a material one indeed, as our own security depended on it. The troops were sent out too late, the Rebels were at least two months (ahead of) us, and your Lordship would be astonished to see the tract of country they have entrenched and fortified; their number is great, so many hands have been employed.

We are here, to use a common expression, taking the bull by the horns, attacking the enemy in their strong parts. I wish this cursed place was burned. The only use is its harbour which may be said to be material, but in all other respects it is the worst place to act offensively from, or defensively. I have before wrote to your Lordship my opinion that a large army must at length be employed to reduce these people, and mentioned the hiring of foreign troops. I fear it must come to that, or else to avoid a land war and make use only of your fleet.

As usual, the British government didn't pay much attention to Gage and his fears. The royal governor, meanwhile, was bottled up in Boston, surrounded by a hostile and awakened countryside. Colonials dug in around the edges of the city, keeping pressure on the regulars and their Tory supporters.

"Yankee Doodle"

Even before the Revolutionary War began, the British soldiers and the colonists ridiculed each other. Richard Schuchburg, a surgeon in the British Army, wrote a ditty to poke fun at the colonials during the French and Indian War. "Yankee" was an insult, and "doodle" was a slang term for "fool." "Macaroni" was the very fancy trim on British uniforms (gold braid, ribbons, etc.). "Hasty pudding" was basically thick corn meal mush. The tune was old even when Schuchburg wrote his lyrics. But the ridicule backfired. The Yankees liked the song and sang it throughout the Revolution. The final joke was on the British.

"Yankee Doodle"

Yankee Doodle went to town, Riding on a pony;
Stuck a feather in his hat And called it Macaroni.

(Chorus)

Yankee Doodle keep it up, Yankee Doodle dandy;
Mind the music and the step, And with the girls be handy.

Father and I went down to camp Along with Captain Good'in,
And there we saw the men and boys As thick as hasty puddin'.

(*Chorus*)

And there we saw a thousand men, As rich as Squire David;
And what they wasted ev'ry day, I wish it could be sav'ed.

(*Chorus*)

And there I saw a little keg, Its head all made of leather,
They knocked on it with little sticks, To call the folks together.

(*Chorus*)

And there was Captain Washington Upon a slapping stallion,
A-giving orders to his men; I guess there was a million.

(*Chorus*)

And the ribbons on his hat, They looked so very fine, ah!
I wanted peskily to get To give to my Jemima.

(*Chorus*)

And there I saw a swamping gun, Large as a log of maple,
Upon a mighty little cart; A load for father's cattle.

(*Chorus*)

And every time they fired it off, It took a horn of powder;
It made a noise like father's gun, Only a nation louder.

(*Chorus*)

The troopers, too, would gallop up And fire right in our faces;
It scared me almost half to death To see them run such races.

(*Chorus*)

It scared me so I hooked it off, Nor stopped as I remember,
Nor turned about till I got home, Locked up in mother's
chamber.

There are other mocking versions, including the following verse:

I cannot tell you all I saw—They kept up such a smother.
I took my hat off, made a bow, And scampered home to mother.

(Chorus)

The British were trapped in Boston by colonial troops. Other Americans under the leadership of Ethan Allen ventured to Fort Ticonderoga on the New York side of Lake Champlain. Ticonderoga was a two-fold prize. It was placed strategically on the vital water route from New York to Canada. It was also well-equipped with military stores that would serve the colonists well in the coming war.

In an attack on May 10, 1775, the Americans captured the fort, which was defended by a mere 45 regulars, some of them ill or old. The fort had also been providing shelter for two dozen of their wives and children. The dawn attack surprised all the British (except the sentries) in their beds.

Allen wasn't willing to share his leadership with Colonel Benedict Arnold, who accompanied him on the raid. Arnold finally agreed to march with Allen at the head of the troops but to refrain from issuing any orders to Allen's Green Mountain Boys. Ethan Allen:

> ...directions were privately sent to me from... Connecticut, to raise the Green Mountain Boys and, if possible, with them to surprise and take the fortress, Ticonderoga. This enterprise I cheerfully undertook and...made a forced march from Bennington, and arrived at the lake opposite Ticonderoga on the evening of the ninth day of May, 1775, with two hundred and

thirty valiant Green Mountain Boys; and it was with the utmost difficulty that I procured boats to cross the lake. However, I landed eighty-three men near the garrison and sent the boats back for the rear guard. . . But the day had began to dawn, and I found myself under the necessity to attack the fort before the rear guard could cross the lake. . .

(He addressed those of his men who had already crossed the lake):

"Friends and fellow soldiers. . . .your valor has been famed abroad. . .we must this morning either quit our pretensions to valor, or possess ourselves of this fortress in a few minutes. And inasmuch as it is a desperate attempt, which none but the bravest of men dare undertake, I do not urge it on any contrary to his will. You that will undertake voluntarily, poise your firelocks."

The capture of Fort Ticonderoga shows Ethan Allen demanding Captain Delaplace to surrender.

The men being at this time drawn up in three ranks, each poised his firelock. I . . . marched them immediately to the wicket-gate. . .where I found a sentry posted, who instantly snapped his fusee at me. I ran immediately towards him, and he retreated through the covered way into the parade within the garrison, gave a halloo, and ran under a bomb-proof.

. . .the garrison being asleep, except the sentries, we gave three huzzas, which greatly surprised them. One of the sentries made a pass at one of my officers with a charged bayonet and slightly wounded him. . . .(I) demanded of him the place where the commanding officer slept. He showed me a pair of steps in the front of a barrack. . .to which I immediately repaired and ordered the commander, Captain de la Place, to come forth instantly, or I would sacrifice the whole garrison; at which the Captain came immediately to the door, with his breeches in his hand. When I ordered him to deliver to me the fort instantly, he asked me by what authority I demanded it. I answered him, "In the name of the great Jehovah, and the Continental Congress."

The authority of the Congress being very little known at that time, he began to speak again. but I interrupted him, and with my drawn sword over his head, again demanded an immediate surrender of the garrison; to which he then complied and ordered his men to be forthwith paraded without arms, as he had given up the garrison. In the mean time some of my officers had given orders, and in consequence thereof, sundry of the barrack doors were beaten down and about one-third of the garrison imprisoned. . .

This surprise was carried into execution in the grey of the tenth day of May, 1775. The sun seemed to rise that morning with a superior lustre; and Ticonderoga and its dependencies smiled on its conquerors, who tossed about the flowing bowl, and wished success to Congress, and the liberty and freedom of America.

On the British side of the issue stood Lieutenant Jocelyn Feltham, of His Majesty's 26th Foot, who was second in command at the fort to Captain Delaplace. Asleep on the upper floor of the garrison, Feltham was awakened at about 3:30 in the morning by the commotion. Jocelyn Feltham:

> I was awakened by numbers of shrieks and the words, "No quarter, no quarter," from a number of armed rabble. I jumped up,. . .and ran undressed to knock at Captain Delaplace's door and to receive his orders or to wake him. The door was fast. The room I lay in being close to Captain Delaplace's, I stepped back, put on my coat and waistcoat and returned to his room, there being no possibility of getting to the men, as there were numbers of the rioters on the bastions of the wing of the fort, on which the door of my room and back door of Captain Delaplace's room led.

> With great difficulty I got into his room. . .I asked Captain Delaplace, who was now just up, what I should do, and offered to force my way, if possible, to our men. On opening (the) door, the bottom of the stairs was filled with the rioters and many were forcing their way up, knowing the commanding officer lived there. . . .

> From the top of the stairs I endeavored to make them hear me, but it was impossible. On making a signal not to come up the stairs, they stopped and proclaimed silence among themselves. I then addressed them, but in a style not agreeable to them. I asked a number of questions, expecting to amuse them till our people fired, which I must certainly own I thought would have been the case. After asking them the most material questions I could think, viz. by what authority they entered

His Majesty's fort, who were the leaders, what their intent, etc., I was informed by one Ethan Allen and one Benedict Arnold that they had a joint command, Arnold informing me he came from instructions received from the Congress at Cambridge, which he afterward showed me.

Mr. Allen told me his orders were from the province of Connecticut and that he must have immediate possession of the fort and all the effects of George, the Third (those were his words), Mr. Allen insisting on this with a drawn sword over my head and numbers of his followers' firelocks presented at me, alleging I was commanding officer and to give up the fort, and if it was not complied with, or that there was a single gun fired in the fort, neither man, woman or child should be left alive. . .

Mr. Arnold begged it in a genteel manner, but without success; it was owing to him they were prevented getting into Captain Delaplace's room, after they found I did not command. Captain Delaplace, being now dressed, came out. . .

When the commander realized to his embarrassment that the fort had been taken with all but the sentries in bed, he surrendered.

Meanwhile, Governor Gage, Percy, and the others in Boston were trying to cope with shortages of food and other daily necessities as well as the noose tightening around the town. One of those who was stuck in Boston was the crown's tax commissioner Henry Hulton, brother to our Loyalist Lady Ann Hulton. Henry Hulton:

For these two months past our situation has been critical and alarming, the town being blockaded, and the whole country in arms all around us. The people have not only cut us off from any supplies, but they do their utmost to prevent any kind of provision being

42

brought us from the neighboring ports; and as we were surprised into these circumstances, I wonder we have held out so long as we have done. We have bread, salt meat, and fresh fish, and there appears no distress for want of subsistence.

Colonial soldiers were flocking to Boston to "get in on the action." One of those who answered the call was John Trumbull, son of the governor of Connecticut and later renowned as a painter. John Trumbull:

The entire army, if it deserved the name, was but an assemblage of brave, enthusiastic, undisciplined country lads; the officers, in general, quite as ignorant of military life as the troops, excepting a few elderly men, who had seen some irregular service among the provincials. . . Our first occupation was to secure our positions, by constructing fieldworks for defense.

In his voluminous diary, Trumbull remembered one form of training that proved disastrous.

Nothing of military importance occurred for some time; the enemy occasionally fired upon our working parties, whenever they approached too nigh to their works; and in order to familiarize our raw soldiers to this exposure, a small reward was offered in general orders, for every ball fired by the enemy, which should be picked up and brought to headquarters. This soon produced the intended effect—a fearless emulation among the men; but it produced also a very unfortunate result; for when the soldiers saw a ball, after having struck and rebounded from the ground several times (en ricochet) roll sluggishly along, they would run and place a foot before it, to stop it, not aware that a heavy ball long retains sufficient impetus to overcome such an obstacle. The consequence was, that several brave lads lost their feet, which were crushed by weight of the rolling shot. The order was of course withdrawn, and they were cautioned against touching a ball, until it was entirely at rest. One thing had been ascertained by this means, the caliber of the enemy's guns—eighteen pounds. Thirteen inch shells were also occasionally fired, some of which exploded at first, to our no small annoyance and alarm; but some of these also being picked up (having failed of igniting) were carried to headquarters, and by this means their dimensions were also ascertained.

Shortly, the encircling colonials heard rumors that the enemy planned to fortify the harbor and move to oust the rebels from the hills around Boston on June 18. On the morning of June 17, 1775, the British awakened to discover that the rebels had hastily dug

The American troops built their redoubt on Breed's Hill, by Bobbetts

44

fortifications on the Charlestown hills above the harbor. A force of British regulars under General Sir William Howe set out to dislodge them. Misnamed "The Battle of Bunker Hill," it was actually fought on the adjacent Breeds Hill. The British advanced three times and were pushed back twice. The colonials' supply of ammunition falling low, their commander Colonel William Prescott ordered, "Don't fire till you see the whites of their eyes!"

One of those who served at Bunker Hill was Private Peter Brown, a company clerk from the Massachusetts town of Westford, who wrote to his mother about the battle. Peter Brown:

> Friday, the sixteenth of June we were ordered to parade at six o'clock with one day's provisions and blankets ready for a march somewhere, but we did not know where. So we readily and cheerfully obeyed. . . . About nine o'clock at night we marched down to Charlestown Hill.
>
> . . .we entrenched and made a fort of about ten rod long and eight wide, with a breastwork of about eight more. We worked there undiscovered till about five in the morn, and then we saw our danger, being against eight ships of the line and all Boston fortified against us.
>
> . . . And about half after five in the morn, we not having about half the fort done, they began to fire (I suppose as soon as they had orders) pretty briskly a few minutes, and then stopped, and then again to the number of about twenty or more. They killed one of us, and then they ceased till about eleven o'clock, and then they began pretty brisk again; and that caused some of our young country people to desert, apprehending the danger in a clearer manner than the rest, who were more diligent in digging and fortifying our-

45

selves against them. We began to be almost beat out, being tired by our labor and having no sleep the night before, but little victuals, no drink but rum . . .

. . .They fired very warm from Boston and from on board, till about two o'clock when they began to fire from the ships in the ferryway [between Boston and Charlestown] and from the ship that lay in the river against the Neck to stop our reinforcements, which they did in some measure. . . .Our officers sent time after time after the cannon from Cambridge in the morning and could get but four, the captain of which fired but a few times and then swang his hat round three times to the enemy, then ceased to fire.

It being about three o'clock, there was a little cessation of the cannons roaring. Come to look, there was a matter of forty barges full of regulars coming over to us. It is supposed there were about three thousand of them and about seven hundred of us left not deserted, besides five hundred reinforcement that could not get so nigh to us as to do any good hardly, till they saw we must all be cut off, or some of them, and then they advanced.

When our officers saw that the regulars would land, they ordered the artillery to go out of the fort and prevent their landing, if possible, from which the artillery captain took his pieces and went right off home to Cambridge as fast as he could, for which he is now confined and we expect will be shot for it.

But the enemy landed and fronted before us and formed themselves in an oblong square, so as to surround us which they did in part, and after they were well formed, they advanced towards us in order to swallow us up. But they found a chokey mouthful of us, though we could do nothing with our small arms as yet for distance and had but two cannon and nary gunner.

And they from Boston and from the ships a-firing and throwing bombs keeping us down till they got almost round us.

On the third British advance, the Americans fell back and retreated. Although technically a loss for the colonies, the British suffered more than twice as many casualties as the defenders. Because the battle took place in full view of the higher points of Boston (including rooftops), many citizens watched the action. One of those was Henry Hulton:

The country is very strong by nature, and the rebels have possessed themselves of all the advantageous posts, and have thrown up entrenchments in many parts. From the heights of this place, we have a view of the whole town, the harbor, and country round about for a great extent, and last Saturday I was spectator of a most awful scene my eyes ever beheld. On the morning of the 17th, it was observed that the rebels had thrown up a breast-work, and were preparing to open a battery upon the Heights above Charlestown, from whence they might incommode the shipping, and destroy the north part of Boston. Immediately a cannonading began from the battery in the north part of the town and the ships of war, on those works, and on the enemy wherever they could be discovered within reach of their guns. Soon after eleven o'clock, the grenadiers, light infantry, marines, and two battalions marched out of their encampments, and embarked in boats, and before high water were landed on a point of land to the eastward of Charlestown, and they immediately took post on a little eminence. . . .the whole advanced, some on the other side, round the hill where the battery was erected, and some through part of Charlestown. On that side of the hill which was not visible from Boston, it seems very strong lines were thrown up, and were occupied by many thousands of the rebels. The troops advanced with great ardor towards the intrenchments....many brave officers and men were killed and wounded. As soon as they got to the intrenchments, the rebels fled, and many of them were killed in the trenches and in their flight.

Upon the firing from the houses, the town was immediately set in flames, and at four o'clock, we saw the fire and the sword, all the horrors of war raging. The town was burning all through the night....Dear was the purchase of our safety! In the evening the streets were filled with the wounded and the dying; the sight of which, with the lamentations of the women and children over their husbands and fathers, pierced one to the soul.

The beleaguered British held out in Boston for several more months. During the winter of 1775-1776, after George Washington had been named Commander in Chief of the American forces, Henry Knox was commissioned Colonel of Artillery. Cannon and the like, however, were in short supply. Knox, with Washington's approval, took a troop of soldiers to Ticonderoga, still in American hands. From that remote outpost, Knox and his command dragged the 43 cannons and 16 mortars captured by Ethan Allen (and Benedict Arnold) overland through a New England winter to Boston. There, the artillery were used to fortify yet another hill near the city, Dorchester Heights.

With that, the British gave up and evacuated Boston on March 17, 1776. The evacuees straggled to the safe harbors of Canada. Loyalist Lady Ann Hulton had fled to England some months before but reported in a letter of her brother's arrival in Halifax, Nova Scotia. Ann Hulton:

By the latest Accounts from Boston The Town was still invirond by the Enemy, who were urged to make a general attack upon it, (by a deputation from the Congress). They had often threatend it and made some efforts....They are numerous but in a wretched condition, in Rags, dirt, and vermin... (Chester, England, January 17, 1776)

Two or three days ago I rec'd a Letter from my Brother dated Halifax, April 19, 1776. he says "after all our Perils and troubles we are thank God got safe to this place and my family are in health.

"It is wonderful how we have been preserved thro' all our alarms, Dangers, and distresses. We suffer in loss of property with many worthy persons, here alas! are many families who lived in ease and plenty at Boston, that now have scarce a shelter, or any means of subsistence. however the fugitives in general seem to bear their Adversity with great fortitude." (Wem, England, June 14, 1776)

Bullseye!

From a Fight for Justice to a War of Independence

The British had left New England. The conflict was spreading around the colonies. King George III and Parliament couldn't ignore the situation or hope it would just go away. The colonists, on the other hand, needed supplies and other support from overseas. Yet other countries were reluctant to aid them, since it was still not clear that the colonies were actually seeking independence from Britain. In fact, on July 5, 1775, the Second Continental Congress had sent an appeal to the King for an end to military hostilities and a peaceful solution to their difficulties. Called the Olive Branch Petition, it was, like Thomas Gage, ignored.

To prevent foreign powers from helping the rebels, Parliament passed a Prohibitory Act in early 1776. This law forbade all communication with the rebel colonies and declared a blockade of the Atlantic coast. The move placed a wedge between the colonies and the Mother Country that pushed the Americans further along the road toward independence.

The British took another fateful step that spring. Since they couldn't gather enough British soldiers to send to the colonies, they hired Hessians from Germany and sent them to America. The colonists were furious, and that anger gave greater voice to radicals who were clamoring for independence.

One of those who spoke was Thomas Paine. Although a recent immigrant from England, he immediately took up the cause for freedom. His pamphlet "Common Sense" was passed among nearly all of the colonists who could read, hundreds of thousands of them. This was a turning point in the Revolution. A portion of that stirring essay is reprinted here. Thomas Paine:

In the following pages I offer nothing more than simple facts, plain arguments, and common sense; and have no other preliminaries to settle with the reader, than that he will divest himself of prejudice....

Volumes have been written on the subject of the struggle between England and America. Men of all ranks have embarked in the controversy, from different motives, and with various designs; but all have been ineffectual, and the period of debate is closed. Arms as the last resource decide the contest; the appeal was

Drawing of German soldiers being drafted to fight for the British in America, by Darley

the choice of the king, and the continent has accepted the challenge.

The sun never shined on a cause of greater worth. 'Tis not the affair of a city, a county, a province, or a kingdom; but of a continent—of at least one eighth part of the habitable globe. 'Tis not the concern of a day, a year, or an age; posterity are virtually involved in the contest, and will be more or less affected even to the end of time, by the proceedings now. Now is the seed-time of continental union, faith and honor. The least fracture now will be like a name engraved with the point of a pin on the tender rind of a young oak; the wound would enlarge with the tree, and posterity read it in full grown characters.

I have heard it asserted by some, that as America has flourished under her former connection with Great Britain, the same connection is necessary towards her future happiness, and will always have the same effect. Nothing can be more fallacious than this kind of argument. We may as well assert that because a child has thrived upon milk, that it is never to have meat, or that the first twenty years of our lives is to become a precedent for the next twenty. But even this is admitting more than is true; for I answer roundly, that America would have flourished as much, and probably much more, had no European power taken any notice of her. The commerce by which she hath enriched herself are the necessities of life, and will always have a market while eating is the custom of Europe.

But (England) has protected us, say some. That she hath engrossed us is true, and defended the continent at our expense as well as her own, is admitted; and she would have defended Turkey from the same motive, (which is to say) for the sake of trade and dominion.

But Britain is the parent country, some say. Then the more shame upon her conduct. Even brutes do not devour their young, nor savages make war upon their families; wherefore, the assertion, if true, turns to her reproach; but it happens not to be true. . . Europe, and not England, is the parent country of America. This new world hath been the asylum for the persecuted lovers of civil and religious liberty from every part of Europe. Hither have they fled, not from the tender embraces of the mother, but from the cruelty of the monster; and it is so far true of England, that the same tyranny which drove the first emigrants from home pursues their descendents still.

But, admitting that we were all of English descent, what does it amount to? Nothing. Britain, being now an open enemy, extinguishes every other name and title; and to say that reconciliation is our duty, is truly farcical. The first king of England, of the present line (William the Conqueror) was a Frenchman, and half the peers (noblemen) of England are descendants from the same country; wherefore, by the same method of reasoning, England ought to be governed by France.

Europe is too thickly planted with kingdoms to be long at peace, and whenever a war breaks out between England and any foreign power, the trade of America goes to ruin, because of her connection with Britain. The next war may not turn out like the last, and should it not, the advocates for reconciliation now will be wishing for separation then, because neutrality in that case would be a safer convoy than a man of war. Everything that is right or reasonable pleads for separation. The blood of the slain. . .cries 'TIS TIME TO PART.

Many rebels were not at all sure that they wanted a split from England. Even if they did, what form would the new government take? One of those uncertain was

Abigail Adams, the wife of John Adams of Massachusetts (later President Adams). John was away from their home a lot during those fateful years, at the Continental Congresses and other meetings. While this made life difficult for Abigail, we today are fortunate that they were both letter writers. The letters they left behind give a clear picture of the doubts many colonists had.

Abigail wrote to John on November 27, 1775, when he was in Philadelphia. Abigail Adams:

> I wish I knew what mighty things were fabricating. If a form of government is to be established here, what one will be assumed? Will it be left to our assemblies to choose one? And will not many men have many minds? And shall we not run into dissensions among ourselves? . . .
>
> I am more and more convinced that man is a dangerous creature; and that power, whether vested in many or a few, is ever grasping, and, like the grave, cries "Give, Give." The great fish swallow up the small . . .
>
> The reins of government have been so long slackened that I fear the people will not quietly submit to those restraints which are necessary for the peace and security of the community. If we separate from Britain, what code of laws will be established? How shall we be governed so as to retain our liberties? Can any government be free which is not administered by general stated laws? Who shall frame these laws? Who will give them force and energy? It is true your resolutions, as a body, have hitherto had the force of laws; but will they continue to have?
>
> When I consider these things, and the prejudices of people in favor of ancient customs and regulations, I feel anxious for the fate of our monarchy or democracy, or whatever is to take place.

John Adams, for his part, spent that winter and spring in Philadelphia, struggling over some of the same questions. By early summer, the die was cast. On July 3, 1776, he wrote to his wife in Quincy. John Adams:

Yesterday the greatest question was decided which ever was debated in America, and a greater, perhaps, never was nor will be decided among men. A resolution was passed without one dissenting colony, "that the United Colonies are, and of right ought to be, free and independent States, and as such they have, and of right ought to have, full power to make war, conclude peace, establish commerce, and to do all other acts and things which other States may rightfully do." You will see in a few days a Declaration setting forth the causes which have impelled us to this mighty revolution, and the reasons which will justify it in the sight of God and man. A plan of confederation will be taken up in a few days.

. . . I am surprised at the suddenness as well as greatness of this revolution. Britain has been filled with folly, and America with wisdom. At least, this is my judgment. Time must determine.

It is the will of Heaven that the two countries should be sundered forever. . . . The second day of July, 1776, will be the most memorable. . . in the history of America. I am apt to believe that it will be celebrated by succeeding generations as the great anniversary festival. It ought to be commemorated as the day of deliverance, by solemn acts of devotion to God Almighty. It ought to be solemnized with pomp and parade, with shows, games, sports, guns, bells, bonfires and illuminations, from one end of this continent to the other, from this time forward, forevermore.

John Adams was only off by two days. In America the annual celebration with bells, fireworks, games, sports, pomp and parade takes place on the Fourth of July, known as Independence Day. On July 4, 1776, the Continental Congress at Philadelphia approved the Declaration of Independence written by Thomas Jefferson and others. The opening words are as ringing today as they were more than two centuries ago.

Declaration of Independence (Excerpt)

When, in the course of human events, it becomes necessary for one people to dissolve the political bands which have connected them with another, and to assume, among the powers of the earth, the separate and equal station to which the laws of nature and of nature's God entitle them, a decent respect to the opinions of mankind requires that they should declare the causes which impel them to the separation.

We hold these truths to be self-evident, that all men are created equal, that they are endowed by their Creator with certain unalienable rights, that among these are life, liberty, and the pursuit of happiness. That, to secure these rights, governments are instituted among men, deriving their just powers from the consent of the governed. That, whenever any form of government becomes destructive of these ends, it is the right of the people to alter or to abolish it, and to institute new government, laying its foundation on such principles, and organizing its powers in such form, as to them shall seem most likely to effect their safety and happiness.

Timetable

Definitions

bastion - projection from a fortification

breeches - knee pants

breastworks - low wall to protect gunners

Declaratory Act - Law passed by Parliament in 1766 after the Stamp Act was repealed. Stated that the British government had the right to make and enforce laws binding on the colonists "in all cases whatsoever" although the colonists weren't represented in Parliament.

fusee - cannon fuse

garrett - attic

grenadiers - artillery soldiers chosen for size and strength

Intolerable Acts - (Coercive Acts) A series of laws passed by Parliament in 1774. The Boston Port Bill closed that harbor. The Massachusetts Government Act banned town meetings.

light infantry - foot soldiers

man of war - armed navy ship

manse - minister's home; parsonage

mortar - short-barreled cannon that fired high shells

Quartering Act - Laws passed in 1765 and 1774 requiring the colonists to provide food and housing for British soldiers in America. One of the Intolerable Acts.

regulars - British army

rod - measure of distance equaling 5½ yards

Sons of Liberty - secret patriotic organization founded in 1765 to oppose the Stamp Act

Stamp Act - Law passed in 1765 that taxed all legal documents, newspapers, pamphlets and other such documents issued in the colonies.

Sugar Act - Law passed in 1764 placing customs duties on sugar, coffee, wine, textiles and other goods imported into the American colonies.

surtout - overcoat

Tea Act - Law passed in 1773 removing export duties on tea. It allowed the British East India Company to sell tea directly to the colonists at a cheaper rate than the American merchants could meet. Protests reached a high point with the Boston Tea Party.

Tory - colonist loyal to the king

Townshend Acts - Laws passed in 1767 by Parliament to raise money in the colonies. Customs duties were placed on glass, paper, tea, lead and paint. All but the tax on tea were repealed in 1770.

victuals - food

whig - supporter of the Revolution

Places to Visit

Boston - Many sites associated with "The Shot Heard 'Round the World" are linked today in Boston by a route called the Freedom Trail: the Paul Revere House, the Old North Church and the site of the Boston Massacre and the Bunker Hill Monument. 1-800-888-5515

Concord - The Old Manse, home of Rev. William Emerson hard by the bridge, is open to the public from spring through fall. 508-369-3909

Lexington - The local historical society owns Buckman Tavern, Monroe Tavern (both buildings saw action that April dawn) and the Hancock-Clarke House. 617-862-1703

The Museum of Our National Heritage has regular exhibits of historic interest. 617-861-6559

Minuteman National Historic Park - in Lexington and Concord, commemorates the events of April 19, 1775. An auto road follows Battle Road from Lexington Common to the North Bridge in Concord, with major exhibits at visitors centers. 508-369-6993

Fort Ticonderoga - The fort, in upstate New York, is a national historic landmark with a museum, artillery demonstrations and fife and drum performances. 518-585-2821

Philadelphia - Independence National Historical Park at Independence Square, marks the place where the Declaration of Independence was first read in public. Independence Hall was the site of the Second Continental Congress in 1775 and 1776. 215-597-8974

Virginia - Colonial Williamsburg is an elaborate re-creation of the capitol of Virginia from 1699-1780. Many events and buildings explore the colonial and revolutionary experience. 1-800-447-8679

Bibliography

The Almanac of American History, Arthur M. Schlesinger, Jr., general editor. New York: Putnam Publishing Group, 1983.

American Heritage Songbook, by the editors of American Heritage. New York: American Heritage Publishing Co., Inc., 1969.

Annals of America, volume 2, 1755-1783, "Resistance and Revolution." Chicago: Encyclopedia Britannica, Inc., 1968.

Brand, Oscar, *Songs of '76*. New York: M. Evans and Company, Inc., 1972.

Churchill, Winston S., *The Age of Revolution*, (volume 3, "A History of the English Speaking People"). New York: Dodd, Mead & Company, 1962.

The Colonies and the New Nation, edited by Richard B. Morris and James Woodress, (vol. 1, "Voices from America's Past"). New York: E. P. Dutton & Co., Inc., 1963.

Emerson, William, *Diaries and Letters of William Emerson, 1743-1776*. Arranged by Amelia Forbes Emerson [np, sn], 1972.

Evening Entertainment, Containing airs, songs, dances, hornpipes, cotillions, reels, waltzes and marches for the German flute or violin. Second edition. Baltimore: J. Carrs Music Store, 1797.

Fisher, David Hackett, *The Midnight Ride of Paul Revere*. New York: Oxford University Press, 1994.

Home Book of Verse. New York: Holt, Rinehart and Winston, 1953.

Hulton, Ann, *Letters of a Loyalist Lady*. Cambridge: Harvard University Press, 1927.

Lister, Jeremy, *Concord Fight*. Cambridge: Harvard University Press, 1931.

Paul Revere's Three Accounts of His Famous Ride, with an introduction by Edmund S. Morgan. Boston: A Revolutionary War Bicentennial Commission and Massachusetts Historical Society Publication, 1967.

Rankin, Hugh F., *The American Revolution*. New York: G. P. Putnam's Sons, 1964.

Scheer, George F. and Hugh F. Rankin, *Rebels and Redcoats*. New York: World Publishing, 1957.

Silverman, Jerry, *The American History Songbook*. Pacific, MO: Melbay Publications, Inc., 1992.

"We Were There!" April 19, 1775, The American Rebels. Copyright 1975 by Vincent J-R Kehoe, mimmeographed.

Yanak, Ted and Pam Cornelison, *The Great American History Fact-Finder*. Boston and New York: Houghton Mifflin Company, 1993.

Additional Reading for Students

Fast, Howard, *April Morning*. New York: Crown Publishers, Inc., 1961.

Finlayson, Ann, *Rebecca's War*. New York: Frederick Warne and Company, Inc., 1972.

Fischer, David Hackett, *Paul Revere's Ride*. New York: Oxford University Press, 1994.

Forbes, Esther, *Johnny Tremain*. Boston: Houghton, Mifflin, 1971.

—————— *Paul Revere and the World He Lived In*. Boston: Houghton Mifflin, 1942.

Lexington, Concord and Bunker Hill, The Editors of American Heritage and Francis Russell. New York: American Heritage Publishing Co., Inc., 1963.

Marks, Katherine, *Away to Fundy Bay*. Walker, 1985.

Tourtellot, Arthur Bernon, *William Diamond's Drum*. Garden City, NY: Doubleday and Company, 1959.

About the Author

Jeanne Munn Bracken wears two professional hats—writer and librarian. Her work at the reference desk of two libraries in suburban Boston for the past sixteen years has triggered her interest in the events covered in *The Shot Heard 'Round the World: The Beginnings of the American Revolution*. She has also been a guide at the home of Ralph Waldo Emerson in Concord. She has been a columnist for the Littleton (MA) *Independent* for fifteen years and has written numerous articles and commentaries that have been published in newspapers and magazines from coast to coast. Her books include *Children with Cancer* (Oxford University Press, 1986) and *It All Began With an Apple* (history of the Veryfine Products juice company), 1988 and 1994 editions. She lives in Littleton, Massachusetts, with her husband, two daughters, and four cats.